Getting started

Content

In the first manual your Learner was introduced to a phonic approach to re[…] They should now feel confident with single-letter sounds and some letter c[…]nd sounds together to make words. They should also know some words by sig[…]ort sentences.

The Sounds Chart on the following pages show which sounds are covered in this manual.
It is essential that your Learner has already completed the first manual before starting this one.

In this manual your Learner will build on their phonic knowledge and learn different letter combinations that represent vowel sounds such as ***ay***, ***ai***, ***ee***, ***ea***, ***y***, ***oa***, ***ow*** and ***ar****.* We call these **long vowels**.

In this manual the **long vowel sounds** are shown (only on the Mentor pages) with a short line above the letter like this: **ā, ē, ī, ō, ū** to remind you how to pronounce these sounds. It is very important for your Learner to **hear** the difference between a **long vowel** sound, ***ā*** as in d**ay**, r**ai**n and a **short vowel** sound ***a*** as in **a**pple, c**a**t without saying the letter names.

Understanding and using this Complex Code is a big step for many Learners and they may need extra time and support.

Learners will also learn:

1. More Sight Words
2. Word endings such as **ing**, **ed**
3. Simple punctuation as an aid to reading: full stops, question marks

Sounds covered in this manual.

Sound	Example	Example	Example
a	c**a**t		
b	**b**un		
c	**c**ow	lu**ck**	**k**ite
d	**d**og	a**dd**	
e	l**e**g		
f	**f**at	sti**ff**	
g	ba**g**	e**gg**	
h	**h**and		
i	**i**n		
j	**j**ug		
l	**l**ip	fu**ll**	
m	**m**en		
n	**n**ot		
o	p**o**t		
p	ho**p**		

Sounds covered in this manual.

Sound	Example	Example	Example
qu	**qu**ick		
r	**r**ib		
s	**s**un	me**ss**	
t	**t**op		
u	r**u**n		
v	**v**an		
w	**w**in		
x (ks)	ta**x**		
y	**y**es		
z	**z**ip	ja**zz**	
th	**th**en	mo**th**	
ch	**ch**op	ma**tch**	
sh	ru**sh**		
ng	ra**ng**		
nk	ra**nk**		

Sounds covered in this manual.

Sound	Example	Example	Example
b	ra**bb**it		
m	co**mm**a		
n	su**nn**y		
p	ha**pp**y		
r	ho**rr**id		
t	po**tt**ed		
w	**w**hen		
(Long) ā	r**ai**n	d**ay**	
(Long) ē	tr**ee**	t**ea**	ver**y**
(Long) ō	b**oa**t	gr**ow**	
(Long) ī	m**y**	f**igh**t	
ar	c**ar**d		

In the first manual your Learner was introduced to some high frequency **Sight Words**. New words will be covered in this manual in the same way. Remember, some Learners find it helpful to take a picture of the word in their head.

Sight Words are introduced in small chunks in each manual:

Sight Words already covered					
about	do	her	of	they	would
all	don't	I	out	time	you
are	for	I'm	put	to	
be	go	me	she	was	
could	have	my	the	we	
day	he	no	there	what	

New Sight Words in this manual		
come	where	call
some	when	want
down	who	here
were	give	after
know	your	before

Get started

1. Use the statements on the next page to explain to your Learner what they will be learning in this manual.

2. Remind them that you will cover all the steps in the activities to make sure there are no gaps in their knowledge and they will have plenty of time to repeat and practise activities when they need to.

Tip:

Notes:

Get started

In this manual you will:

Practise letter sounds and blend them to make words.

Understand how letters can be put together to make new sounds.

Understand that some sounds can be spelt in more than one way.

Read word endings such as **ed** and **ing**.

Read some words by sight.

Read longer words and sentences.

You will be asked to **listen**, **look** and **read** aloud.
You can also have a go at writing short words.
There will be lots of chances for you to see how you are getting on and the progress you are making.

Listen and point

Learners are introduced to the **long ā** sound

1. Remind your Learner of the vowel sounds they learned in the first manual: ***a***, ***e***, ***i***, ***o***, ***u*** (as in cat, bed, tin, top, cup).

2. Tell your Learner that there are other vowel sounds that use different letter combinations.
   - Point to the two-letter combinations that make **long ā**: ***ay***, ***ai*** and say the sound.
   - Explain that they are spelt differently but they both make the same **long ā** sound.
   - Read the two lists of words emphasising the **long ā** sound.

3. Now go through the ***ay*** list with your Learner.

4. Point to each word as you read it and ask your Learner to repeat the word.
   - Go through the same list at random, saying the words and ask your Learner to find and point to the correct word in each case.

5. Repeat these activities with the other list: ***ai***

6. Read the other ways to represent the **long ā** shown at the bottom of the page. Explain that these will be covered later in the programme.

Tip: Always pronounce letters that make a long vowel sound as **one sound**, such as **long ā** in pl**ai**n, tr**ay**.

Notes:

The letters in bold say **long a**

ay	**ai**
d**ay**	w**ai**t
s**ay**	p**ai**n
pl**ay**	g**ai**n
tr**ay**	t**ai**l
l**ay**	sn**ai**l
m**ay**	tr**ai**n
g**ay**	**ai**m

Long a can also be spelt as: m**a**d**e**, **eigh**t, gr**ea**t, th**ey**

Listen

Learners listen and identify words with the **long ā** and **short a** sound

Words to read

1. pay
2. van
3. rain
4. rat
5. play
6. train
7. bail
8. patch
9. aim
10. stay

Tip: You may need to repeat the words more than once.

This task is not about spelling – do the writing for your Learner.

1. Tell your Learner to listen to one word at a time and decide whether they can hear the **long *ā*** as in d**ay** or r**ai**n or the **short a** sound as in c**a**t or f**a**n.

2. Say the word **pay** and sound it out: *p-**ay***. Show how this has been recorded on the Learner page.

- Do the same with van: *v-**a**-n*. Show how this has been recorded.

3. Read the next word: **rain.** Sound out the word: *r-**ai**-n*. Say the word again. Ask your Learner:

- Which sound can you hear in the middle of the word **rain?** Is it long ***ā*** or short ***a***.
- Ask your Learner to tick the correct column to show this.
- Write the word for your Learner in the left-hand column.
- Ask your Learner to read the word.

4. Do the same with all the other words.

Notes:

Listen

Listen for the **long a** and **short a**

		Long a	Short a
		ai/ay	a
1.	p**ay**	✓	
2.	v**a**n		✓
3.			
4.			
5.			
6.			
7.			
8.			
9.			
10.			

Listen and point

Learners listen and find the words with the **long ā** and **short a** sound

Words to read

claim
chap
snail
stain
may
pain
pat
had
pay
stay
map
clay

Tip:

1. Tell your Learner that they will need to use their sounding out skills to find the word on the Learner page that matches what they hear.

2. Read the first word: **claim**. Sound it out *c-l-**ai**-m*. Say it again as a whole word.
   Ask your Learner:
   - What is the first sound you can hear? ***c***
   - What is the next sound you can hear? ***l***
   - What is the next sound you can hear? ***ai***
   - What is the last sound you can hear? ***m***

3. Ask your Learner to say the word again blending the sounds: **claim**.
   - Tell them to find the word **claim** in the grid and tick it.

4. Repeat the process with all the other words.

5. Ask your Learner to look at the words and circle all the **long ā** sounds.

Notes:

Listen and point

Find the words with the **long a** and **short a** sound

st**ay**	cl**ai**m	map	cl**ay**
p**ai**n	chap	p**ay**	st**ai**n
m**ay**	had	sn**ai**l	pat

Read and check

Learners practise reading words with the **long ā** and **short a** sounds

1. Ask your Learner to read each word in the grid on the Learner page.
   - Tell them to tick the ones they get right. Leave the others blank.

2. When your Learner has finished, go over any words that have not been ticked.
   - Read each of these words and sound them out.
   - Then ask your Learner to read them again and tick the ones they get right.

3. Make a note of any words that are still a problem in the Notes box.
   - Go over these words again once or twice.
   - If any words remain a problem, or take two or three tries to get right, add them to the blank column on page 21.

Tip: Point out the **ay** letter combination. Tell your Learner it mostly comes at the end of words. This makes it an easy pattern to spot when reading.

Notes:

Read and check

Check that you can read these words with the **long a** and **short a** sounds

ay	✓
pay	
sway	
tray	
jay	
say	
stay	
pray	
gay	
way	
play	
day	
bay	

ai	✓
aim	
Spain	
gain	
faith	
fail	
drain	
snail	
sail	
jail	
wait	
waist	
chain	

a	✓
cat	
fat	
clap	
man	
sad	
catch	
mash	
snack	
that	
sand	
flat	
rang	

Gap fill

Learners complete words that have a **long ā** sound: **ay** or **ai**

Words to read

ay	**ai**
play	pain
lay	bail
ray	tail
pay	claim
tray	raid
stay	chain
stray	train
may	plain
pray	faith

Tip: Cover up the grid not in use. This will help your Learner to focus on the task.

1. Ask your Learner to look at the grid on the left of the Learner page.
- Ask them to read the **long *ā*** sound in the heading: ***ay*** (as in p***ay***).

2. Read the first word: **play**. Sound it out: *p*-*l*-***ay***.
- Show your Learner how to complete the word using the letters given.
- Write in the letters and ask your Learner to read the whole word.

3. Take one word at a time in the **ay** list.
- Read it and sound it out.
- Ask your Learner to use the letters to complete the words in the grid. Encourage them to do the writing.
- You may need to repeat the words more than once.
- Use letter cards so that your Learner can move the letters around. This hands-on approach helps learning.

4. Complete the whole activity again with the words in the **ai** grid.

Notes:

Gap fill

Use the letters to complete words that have a **long a** sound: **ay** or **ai**

ay	
l p	___ ___ **ay**
l	___ **ay**
r	___ **ay**
p	___ **ay**
r t	___ ___ **ay**
s t	___ ___ **ay**
t s r	___ ___ ___ **ay**
m	___ **ay**
r p	___ ___ **ay**

ai	
n p	___ **ai** ___
b l	___ **ai** ___
l t	___ **ai** ___
c m l	___ ___ **ai** ___
r d	___ **ai** ___
ch n	_____ **ai** ___
n t r	___ ___ **ai** ___
p l n	___ ___ **ai** ___
th f	___ **ai** _____

Read and check

Learners practise reading words with the **long ā** sound: **ay, ai**

1. Ask your Learner to read each word in the grid on the Learner page.
   - Tell them to tick all the words they get right. Leave the others blank.

2. When your Learner has finished, go over any words that have not been ticked.
   - Read each of these words and sound them out.
   - Ask your Learner to read them again and tick the ones they get right.

3. Make a note of any words that are still a problem in the Notes box.
   - Go over these words again once or twice.
   - If any words remain a problem, or take two or three tries to get right, add them to the blank column on page 25.

Tip: To help your Learner focus, cover up the column that they are not reading.

Notes:

Read and check

Check that you can read these words with the **long a** sound: **ay, ai**

ay	✓
pay	
gay	
say	
lay	
sway	
stay	
day	
ray	
clay	
tray	
way	
play	
bay	
pray	

ai	✓
tail	
pain	
stain	
pail	
trail	
rail	
chain	
drain	
train	
paint	
faith	
rain	
sail	
plain	

Words from page 17	✓

Gap fill

Learners read sentences and fill in the missing words

1. Explain to your Learner that they will read some sentences that have some words missing. They will choose the right words to complete the sentence.
   - Tell them that they may need to read each sentence more than once to get the meaning.

2. Read out Sentence 1 on the Learner page with the gaps and the words written in brackets:
   It was a ______ ______. (day, bad).
   - Show how to complete the sentence by trying each word from the brackets.
   - Write the correct words in the spaces.
   - Read the sentence again to help your Learner make sense of it: **It was a bad day.**

3. Support your Learner to do the same with the other sentences. Read it with them if needed.
   - Each time ask your Learner to try both words to see which one makes sense.
   - Invite your Learner to write in the words or write for them if they do not feel confident.

Tip: An ESOL Learner may need support to understand the meaning of each sentence. Read the sentences aloud and explain the meaning.

Notes:

Gap fill

Complete these sentences so that they make sense

1.	It was a ___________ ___________.	d**ay**, bad
2.	The man ___________ for the bus in the ___________.	r**ai**n, ran
3.	I ___________ to ___________ fit.	st**ay**, **ai**m
4.	Will you ___________ for the ___________ ticket?	tr**ai**n, p**ay**
5.	The ___________ was to ___________ for them at the pub.	plan, w**ai**t
6.	Fred was sad he could not ___________ in the ___________.	pl**ay**, match
7.	The ___________ dog was on a ___________.	ch**ai**n, mad
8.	He put in a ___________ for his ___________.	p**ay**, cl**ai**m

Read and check

Learners practise reading words with the **long ā** sound: **ay**, **ai**

1. Ask your Learner to read each word in the grid on the Learner page.
- Tell them to tick all the words they get right. Leave the others blank.

2. When your Learner has finished, go over any words that have not been ticked.
- Read each of these words and sound them out.
- Ask your Learner to read them again and tick the ones they get right.

3. Make a note of any words that are still a problem in the Notes box.
- Go over these words again once or twice.
- If any words remain a problem, or take two or three tries to get right, add them to the Parking page (page 61).

Tip:

Notes:

Read and check

Check that you can read these words with the **long a** sound: **ay, ai**

	✓
lay	
sway	
pain	
chain	
say	
plain	
day	
paint	
clay	
tray	
way	
claim	
bay	
rain	

	✓
ray	
wait	
train	
stay	
drain	
sail	
pray	
tail	
gay	
aid	
faith	
play	
paid	
pay	

Words from page 21	✓

Text and check

Learners read sentences that include words with the **long ā** sound: **ay**, **ai**

1. Ask your Learner to read the sentences in the grid.
- Tick all the ones they get right. Leave the others blank.

2. Go over any sentences that have not been ticked.
- Underline any errors in each sentence.
- Read them to your Learner.
- Support your Learner with two-syllable words if they need it. Use a finger to reveal the word bit by bit. Draw in the syllable break with a slash: **sun/set**.
- Ask your Learner to read the sentences again and to tick the ones they get right.

3. Make a note of any words that are a problem in the Notes box. Go over these words again once or twice.

4. If any words remain a problem, or take two or three tries to get right, add them to the Parking page (page 61).

Tip: Ask some questions about the sentences to check understanding, such as: What will happen if I pick up the sack? Who is going to Spain?

Notes:

Text and check

Read some sentences that have words with the **long a** sound: **ay, ai**

	✓
The d**ay** ends with a sunset.	
The man p**ai**d for his tr**ai**n ticket.	
It will have to w**ai**t until p**ay**d**ay**.	
If I pick up that sack I will str**ai**n my back.	
I will pr**ay** for the r**ai**n to stop.	
There was a bank r**ai**d on Sund**ay**.	
The rat's t**ai**l was stuck in the trap.	
Ashok went to Sp**ai**n to st**ay** with his dad.	
I have f**ai**th that you will do what you s**ay**.	

Spot the word

Learners look for the Sight Words: **some**, **come**, **down**, **were**, **know**

This task relies upon whole word recognition.

1. Read the words: **some**, **come**, **down**, **were**, **know** on the Learner page.
- Ask your Learner to read the words.

2. Show your Learner how to search the small boxes for the word **some**.
- Point out that they are looking for a short word beginning with ***s***.
- Tick the word every time you find it. (There are 3.) Write the number on the notepad.

3. Ask your Learner to search the small boxes for the word **come**.
- Tell them it looks like **some** but starts with a ***c***.
- Tick the word. (There are 4.) Write the number on the notepad.

4. Do the same for the other words: **down** (2), **were** (3), **know** (3).

Tip: Ask your Learner to point out things about the words that help them to remember, such as word shape, the beginning of the word or words with a similar spelling pattern.

Notes:

Spot the word

Find these everyday Sight Words

some come down were know

know were some

come come

some some

know

down down

were

come

were come

know

some ______________

come ______________

down ______________

were ______________

know ______________

Read and check

Learners practise reading Sight Words

1. Remind your Learner that the Sight Words in the grid need to be remembered as whole words not sounded out.

2. Ask your Learner to read each word in the grid.
   - Tell them to tick all the words they get right. Leave the others blank.

3. When your Learner has finished go over any words that have not been ticked.
   - Read them to your Learner (**do not** sound them out).
   - Ask your Learner to read them again and tick the ones they get right.

4. If any words remain a problem, or take two or three tries to get right, write them in the Notes box and do 'Look and Say, Copy and Say' (as you do on the Parking page) until your Learner is confident.

Tip:

Notes:

Read and check

Check that you can read these Sight Words

	✓
come	
some	
down	
were	
know	
don't	
they	
were	
some	
time	
come	
all	
were	

	✓
me	
some	
know	
come	
there	
were	
come	
what	
down	
know	
some	
down	
my	

Text and check

Learners read sentences with Sight Words: **some**, **come**, **down**, **were**, **know**

1. Ask your Learner to read the Sight Words: **some**, **come**, **down**, **were**, **know**.
   - Practise the words with your Learner if you need to.

2. Ask your Learner to read the sentences in the grid.
   - Tick all the ones they get right and leave the others blank.

3. Go over any sentences that have not been ticked.
   - Underline any errors in each sentence.
   - Read them to your Learner.
   - Ask your Learner to read the sentences again and to tick the ones they get right.

4. Make a note of any words that are a problem in the Notes box. Go over these words again once or twice.

5. If any words remain a problem, or take two or three tries to get right, add them to the Parking page (page 61).

Tip: Ask some questions about the sentences to check understanding, such as: What's wrong with the van? What can you get from the shop?

Notes:

Text and check

Read some sentences with Sight Words

some **come** **down** **were** **know**

	✓
Did you know the kids were out in the rain?	
I don't know if I can come for the day.	
Put that tray down.	
There are some rubbish films on this time.	
Can you get some muffins from the shop?	
We were up and down the steps all day.	
Come in, sit down and tell us what you know.	
I would add some nutmeg to the mix.	
Can you all come on Sunday?	
My van has some rust on it.	
The lads were on the track.	

Listen and point

Learners are introduced to the **long ē** sound

1. Remind your Learner that there are **short vowel sounds**: ***a***, ***e***, ***i***, ***o, u*** and there are also **long vowel sounds** represented by different letter combinations, such as: ***ai*** and ***ay***.
2. Tell them the next vowel sound they will learn about is **long ē**.
    - Point to the letter combinations that make **long ē**: ***ee***, ***ea*** and say the sound.
    - Explain that they are spelt differently but they both make the same **long ē** sound.
    - Read the two lists of words emphasising the **long ē** sound.
3. Now go through the **ee** list with your Learner:
    - Point to each word as you read it and ask your Learner to repeat the word.
4. Go through the same list at random, saying the words, and ask your Learner to point to the correct word in each case.
5. Repeat these activities with the other list: **ea**.
6. Read the other ways to represent the **long ē** shown at the bottom of the page. Explain that these will be covered later in the programme.

Tip: Always pronounce ***a***, ***e***, ***i***, ***o***, ***u*** as short letter sounds. Do not name these letters. Always pronounce letters that make a long vowel sound as **one sound** such as **long ē**, as in m**ea**n, or k**ee**p.

Notes:

Listen and point

Find the words with the **long e** sound

The letters in bold say **long e**

ee	**ea**
s**ee**	**ea**ch
b**ee**n	r**ea**d
s**ee**n	dr**ea**m
f**ee**l	t**ea**m
sh**ee**p	**ea**st
sw**ee**t	j**ea**ns
sp**ee**ch	d**ea**r

Long e can also be spelt as: happ**y**, ch**ie**f, k**ey**, w**e**, rec**ei**ve, **eve**

Listen

Learners listen and identify words with the **long ē** and **short e** sounds

Words to read

1. sleep
2. fed
3. team
4. free
5. shed
6. men
7. fear
8. pen
9. cheap
10. feed

Tip: You may need to repeat the words more than once.

This task is not about spelling – do the writing for your Learner.

1. Tell your Learner to listen to one word at a time and decide whether they can hear the **long ē** as in d**ee**p or b**ea**m or the **short e** sound as in f**e**d and k**e**pt.

2. Say the word **sleep** and sound it out: *s-l-**ee**-p*. Show how this has been recorded on the Learner page.

- Do the same with the word **fed**: *f-**e**-d.* Show how it has been recorded.

3. Read the next word: **team**. Sound out the word *t-**ea**-m*. Say the word again. Ask your Learner:

- Which sound can you hear in the middle of the word **team**? Is it **long ē** or **short *e***?
- Ask your Learner to tick the correct column to show this.
- Write the word for your Learner in the left-hand column.
- Ask your Learner to read the word.

4. Do the same with all the other words.

Notes:

Listen

Listen for the **long e** and **short e** sounds

		Long e	Short e
		ee/ea	e
1.	sl**ee**p	✓	
2.	fed		✓
3.			
4.			
5.			
6.			
7.			
8.			
9.			
10.			

Listen and point

Learners listen and find the words with the **long ē** and **short e** sounds

Words to read

reach
see
fed
deep
bed
clear
check
bead
cheap
fetch
seed
feed

Tip: Point to **clear**, tell them that when the **long ē**: **ea** sound is followed by **r**, the ***r*** is very soft. Also point out f**e**d and f**ee**d.

1. Tell your Learner that they will use their sounding out skills to find the word on the Learner page that matches what they hear.

2. Read the first word: **reach**. Sound it out *r-**ea**-ch*. Say it again as a whole word. Ask your Learner:
   - What is the first sound you can hear? ***r***
   - What is the next sound you can hear? ***ea***
   - What is the last sound you can hear? ***ch***

3. Ask your Learner to say the word again blending the sounds: **reach**.
   - Tell them to find the word **reach** in the grid and tick it.

4. Repeat the process with all the other words.

5. Ask your Learner to look at the words again and circle all the **long ē** sounds.

Notes:

Listen and point

Find the words with the **long e** and **short e** sounds

b**ea**d	fetch	cl**ea**r	f**ee**d
d**ee**p	check	s**ee**	fed
bed	r**ea**ch	s**ee**d	ch**ea**p

Read and check

Learners practise reading words with the **long ē** sound: **ee**, **ea**, and **short e** sound

1. Ask your Learner to read each word in the grid on the Learner page.

- Tell them to tick all the words they get right. Leave the others blank.

2. When your Learner has finished, go over any words that have not been ticked.

- Read each of these words and sound them out.
- Then ask your Learner to read it again and tick the ones they get right.

3. Make a note of any words that are still a problem in the Notes box.

- Go over these words again once or twice.
- If any words remain a problem, or take two or three tries to get right, add them to the blank column on page 45.

Tip: It may help your Learner if you cover up the columns they are not reading.

Notes:

Read and check

Check that you can read these words with the **long e** and **short e** sounds

ee	✓
see	
been	
sheep	
seen	
speech	
tree	
feel	
deep	
feed	
teeth	
free	
sweet	

ea	✓
eat	
clear	
ear	
read	
fear	
reach	
beast	
clean	
dear	
bead	
mean	
pea	

e	✓
fed	
shell	
pen	
sex	
get	
fetch	
less	
chest	
fell	
help	
shed	
then	

Gap fill

Learners complete words that have a **long ē** sound: **ee, ea**

Words to read

ee	**ea**
free	neat
week	leap
coffee	reach
speech	read
keep	dream
speed	seat
feet	fear
see	each
teeth	cheat

Tip: Cover up the grid not in use. This will help your Learner to focus on the task.

1. Ask your Learner to look at the grid on the left of the Learner page.

2. Ask them to read the **long ē** sound in the heading: ***ee*** (as in tr***ee***).

3. Read the first word: **free**. Sound it out**:** *f-r-**ee***.
   - Show your Learner how to complete the word using the letters given.
   - Write in the letters and ask your Learner to read the whole word.

4. Take one word at a time in the **ee** list.
   - Read it and sound it out.
   - Ask your Learner to use the letters to complete the word in the grid. Encourage them to do the writing.
   - You may need to repeat the words more than once.
   - Use letter cards so that your Learner can move the letters around. This hands-on approach helps learning.

5. Complete the whole activity again with the words in the **ea** grid.

Notes:

Gap fill

Complete the words that have the **long e** sound: **ee, ea**

ee	
r f	__ __ **ee**
k w	__ **ee** __
ff c o	__ __ ___ **ee**
ch s p	__ __ **ee** ___
p k	__ **ee** __
s d p	__ __ **ee** __
f t	__ **ee** __
s	__ **ee**
th t	__ **ee** ___

ea	
n t	__ **ea** __
p l	__ **ea** __
ch r	__ **ea** ___
r d	__ **ea** __
r d m	__ __ **ea** __
t s	__ **ea** __
r f	__ **ea** __
ch	**ea** ___
t ch	___ **ea** __

Read and check

Learners practise reading words with the **long ē** sound: **ee**, **ea**

1. Ask your Learner to read each word in the grid on the Learner page.

- Tell them to tick all the words they get right. Leave the others blank.

2. When your Learner has finished, go over any words that have not been ticked.

- Read each of these words and sound them out.
- Ask your Learner to read them again and tick the ones they get right.

3. Make a note of any words that are still a problem in the Notes box.

- Go over these words again once or twice.
- If any words remain a problem, or take two or three tries to get right, add them to the blank column on page 49.

Tip:

Notes:

Read and check

Check that you can read words with the **long e** sound: **ee, ea**

ee	✓
feed	
queen	
free	
deep	
sleep	
feel	
sheep	
cheek	
speech	
bleed	
street	
need	
seen	
see	

ea	✓
read	
hear	
cheap	
reach	
leaf	
feast	
teach	
deal	
real	
tea	
near	
clean	
dream	
cheat	

Words from page 41	✓

Gap fill

Learners read sentences and fill in the missing words

Your Learner may need to read each sentence more than once to get the meaning.

1. Explain to your Learner they will read some sentences that have some words missing. They will choose the right words to complete the sentence.

2. Read out Sentence 1 with the gaps and the words written in brackets:
I _________ Colin at the _________. (beach, met).
- Show how to complete the sentence by trying each word from the brackets.
- Write the correct words in the spaces.
- Read the sentence again to help your Learner make sense of it: **I met Colin at the beach.**

3. Support your Learner to do the same with the other sentences. Read it with them if needed.
- Each time ask your Learner to try both words to see which one makes sense.
- Invite your Learner to write in the words or write for them if they do not feel confident.

Tip: An ESOL Learner may need support to understand the meaning of each sentence. Read the sentence aloud and explain the meaning.

Notes:

Gap fill

Complete these sentences so that they make sense

1.	I ___________ Colin at the ___________.	b**ea**ch, met
2.	Can you ___________ the ___________?	r**ea**d, scr**ee**n
3.	The ___________ n**ee**ds to ___________.	qu**ee**n rest
4.	The ch**ea**p ___________ are ___________.	best, j**ea**ns
5.	___________ has ___________ to the shops.	b**ee**n, Ben
6.	Can you ___________ me to ___________?	t**ea**ch, r**ea**d
7.	I ___________ well in that ___________.	sl**ee**p, bed
8.	I hear you will be ___________ ___________ Sunday.	next, fr**ee**

Read and check

Learners practise reading words with the **long ē**: **ee**, **ea**

1. Ask your Learner to read each word in the grid on the Learner page.
- Tell them to tick all the words they get right. Leave the others blank.

2. When your Learner has finished, go over any words that have not been ticked.
- Read each of these words and sound them out.
- Ask your Learner to read them again and tick the words they get right.

3. Make a note of any words that are still a problem in the Notes box.
- Go over these words again once or twice.
- If any words remain a problem, or take two or three tries to get right, add them to the Parking page (page 61).

Tip: Point out the spellings for the words: **see** and **sea**. Explain their meaning: I can see the sea.

Notes:

Read and check

Check that you can read these words with the **long e**: **ee, ea**

	✓
read	
sheep	
tea	
sleep	
feel	
mean	
tree	
cheap	
teeth	
dear	
bleed	
pea	
cheek	
each	

	✓
feed	
hear	
weep	
feel	
see	
teach	
been	
meat	
keep	
clean	
dream	
queen	
reach	
sea	

Words from page 45	✓

Text and check

Learners read sentences that include words with the **long ē** sound: **ee**, **ea**

1. Ask your Learner to read the sentences in the grid.
- Tick all the ones they get right. Leave the others blank.

2. Go over any sentences that have not been ticked.
- Underline any errors in each sentence.
- Read them to your Learner.
- Support your Learner with two-syllable words if they need it. Use a finger to reveal the word bit by bit. Draw in the syllable break with a slash: **un/til**.
- Point out that names (people, places, titles) start with a capital letter such as **R**edhill.
- Ask your Learner to read the sentences again and tick the ones they get right.

3. Make a note of any words that are a problem in the Notes box. Go over these words again once or twice.

4. If any words remain a problem, or take two or three tries to get right, add them to the Parking page (page 61).

Tip: Ask some questions about the sentences to check understanding, such as: What sort of cup did the team win? Why did someone keep the sheep?

Notes:

Text and check

Read some sentences that have words with the **long e** sound: **ee**, **ea**

	✓
I had a dr**ea**m that my t**ea**m got the cup for boxing.	
He knows that he n**ee**ds to come **ea**ch day.	
You can t**ea**ch your kids to r**ea**d.	
Come down to Redhill and we will r**ea**ch a d**ea**l.	
I went into a d**ee**p sl**ee**p.	
I hear the sw**ee**ts are ch**ea**p in this shop.	
I could s**ee** you were upset.	
I kept some sh**ee**p for m**ea**t.	
I will not pay you until this is cl**ea**n, is that cl**ea**r?	

Listen and point

Learners read words ending with the **long ē** sound: **y**

1. Tell your Learner that **y** (when found at the end of words with two or more syllables) can also be used to make a **long ē** sound as well as ***ee*** and ***ea*** as shown on the Learner page.

2. Go through the words in the **y** list with your Learner.
- Point to each word as you read it and ask your Learner to repeat the word.
- Emphasise the **long ē** sound at the end of each word: happ***y***, bod***y***.

3. Ask your Learner what is the last sound they can hear in each word: **ē**.
- Point out that this **ē** sound is represented by a **y** in each case.

4. Go through the same list at random. Say the words and ask your Learner to find and point to the correct word in each case.

5. Tell your Learner that these are all two-syllable words.
- Read the words through again with your Learner tapping out the syllables.

Tip: Point out to your Learner that **y** making a **long ē** sound only applies to words that have more than one syllable. In one-syllable words, such as **my, try, fly** the **y** is always pronounced as **long ī** .

Notes:

Listen and point

Listen for the **long e** sound at the end of words: **y**

All the letters in bold say **long e**

ee	**y**	**ea**
s**ee**	happ**y**	**ea**ch
b**ee**n	bod**y**	r**ea**d
s**ee**n	rust**y**	dr**ea**m
f**ee**l	rugb**y**	t**ea**m
sh**ee**p	risk**y**	**ea**st
sw**ee**t	ver**y**	j**ea**ns
sp**ee**ch	curr**y**	d**ea**r

Long e can also be spelt as: ch**ie**f, k**ey**, w**e**, rec**ei**ve, ser**i**ous, **eve**

Gap fill

Learners complete two-syllable words ending in the **long ē** sound: **y**

1. Remind your Learner that the letter **y** makes a **long ē** sound when found at the end of words with two or more syllables.

2. Read the first word in the grid: **body**. Stress the second syllable: **y** (saying **ē**).
   - Repeat the word and ask your Learner to say the whole word.

3. Do the same with the other words across the top row. Each time stress the second syllable and write in a **y** to represent **long ē**.
   - Ask your Learner to complete all the other words in the grid and read each word aloud.
   - Encourage your Learner to do the writing if they feel confident.

Tip: Remind your Learner that **y** making a **long ē** sound only applies to words that have more than one syllable. In one-syllable words, such as **my, try, fly** the **y** is always pronounced as **long *ī***.

Notes:

Gap fill

Use **y** to make the **long e** sound at the end of words

bod**y**	fish __	happ __	curr __
dust __	pit __	smell __	marr __
sand __	itch __	fizz __	grann __
rock __	wind __	chatt __	fogg __
cop __	risk __	sorr __	sill __

Read and check

Learners practise two-syllable words ending in the **long ē** sound: **y**

1. Ask your Learner to read each word in the grid.
- Tell them to tick all the words they get right. Leave the others blank.

2. When your Learner has finished, go over any words that have not been ticked.
- Read each of these words and sound them out.
- Ask your Learner to read the words again and tick the ones they get right.

3. Make a note of any problem words in the Notes box.
- Go over these words again once or twice.
- If any words remain a problem, or take two or three tries to get right, add them to the Parking page (page 61).

Tip:

Notes:

Read and check

Check that you can read these words with the **long e** sound: **y**

	✓
copy	
rusty	
dusty	
misty	
milky	
curry	
itchy	
marry	
risky	
sandy	
silly	
windy	

	✓
chatty	
foggy	
rocky	
fizzy	
body	
pity	
granny	
happy	
smelly	
fishy	
handy	
sorry	

Text and check

Learners read sentences that include words with the **long ē** sound: **ee**, **ea**, **y**

1. Ask your Learner to read the sentences in the grid.
   - Tick all the ones they get right. Leave the others blank.
2. Go over any sentences that have not been ticked.
   - Underline any errors in each sentence.
   - Read them to your Learner.
   - Ask your Learner to read the sentences again and tick the ones they get right.
3. Make a note of any words that are a problem in the Notes box. Go over these words again once or twice.
4. If any words remain a problem, or take two or three tries to get right, add them to the Parking page (page 61).

Tip: Ask some questions about the sentences to check understanding such as: What was the beach like? What was wrong with the fish?

Notes:

Text and check

Read some short sentences that have words with the **long e** sound: **ee**, **ea**, **y**

	✓
I am ver**y** happ**y** to s**ee** you.	
Sall**y** had an itch**y** rash on her ch**ee**k and left **ea**r.	
Harr**y** will you marr**y** me?	
My grann**y** had her t**ea** on a tray.	
Can you get a cop**y** of that for me?	
The b**ea**ch was sand**y** and ver**y** wind**y**.	
The b**ee**f curr**y** is the best.	
Can you r**ea**ch that dust**y** shelf?	
This fish is a bit smell**y**.	

Parking page

Use the page opposite to note down any words you have come across in the manual that your Learner needs to practise again. Do this activity when you have completed all the other activities.

1. Write the words in the first (Park) column as you come across them in the manual.
2. When you and your Learner get to this page:
   - Take **one** word at a time.
   - Read it to your Learner and sound it out. (Note: Sight Words are **not** sounded out.)
   - Ask your Learner to read the whole word.
   - Ask your Learner to copy the word and say it.
   - Tick it if they get it right.
   - Repeat the whole process with the same word. Copy and Say, until they are confident with it. Repeat on a new row if you need to.
3. Repeat the 'Look and Say, Copy and Say' process with all the other words in the Park column.
4. If your Learner continues to struggle with a word, make sure they know what the word means and try putting it into sentences for them.

Tip:

Notes:

Parking page

Park. Look and Say	✓

Copy and Say	✓

Copy and Say	✓

Copy and Say	✓

Parking page

Use the page opposite to note down any words your Learner needs to practise again. Treat in the same way as outlined on the previous Parking page.

Tip:

Notes:

Parking page

Park. Look and Say	✓

Copy and Say	✓

Copy and Say	✓

Copy and Say	✓

Progress check

Explain to your Learner that this is a good point in the programme to see how things are going.

Ask your Learner to read each word in the Progress check.

- Tick everything they get right.
- Leave blank any words that your Learner cannot read.
- Use the Turning Pages Reading Levels to show your Learner how much they have achieved.
- Keep a note of any words or letter sounds they are not confident with. Your Learner can practise them at the beginning of the next session.

Turning Pages Reading Levels

All or most of the words with **long ā** read correctly. (No more than 5 errors.)	**TP Level 2.1**
All or most of the words with **long ē** read correctly. (No more than 5 errors.)	**TP Level 2.2**

Remind your Learner that the levels given are only relevant to Turning Pages. They give a clear picture of their progress and their achievements so far.

Tip:

Notes:

Read and tick all the words you know

Long a	✓
day	
play	
train	
pain	
claim	
bay	
faith	
play	
sway	
aim	

Long a	✓
chain	
paint	
tray	
pay	
aid	
sail	
wait	
paid	
stay	
say	

Long e	✓
feed	
clean	
happy	
teeth	
keep	
team	
hear	
sheep	
body	
speech	

Long e	✓
tree	
risky	
dear	
each	
pity	
jeans	
very	
free	
sorry	
pea	

TP Level 2.1 ☐

TP Level 2.2 ☐

Progress check

Ask your Learner to read each sentence in the Progress check.

- Tick everything they get right.
- Underline any errors in the sentences.
- Use the Turning Pages Reading Levels to show your Learner how much they have achieved.
- Keep a note of any words or letter sounds they are not confident with. Your Learner can practise them at the beginning of the next session.

Turning Pages Reading Levels

All or most of the sentences read correctly. (No more than 5 errors.)	**TP Level 2.3**

If your Learner makes more than 15 errors overall (in both words and sentences) **you will need to go over the relevant activities again and spend some more time practising with the Turning Pages reading books. When you have done this, try the Progress check again.**

Tip:

Notes:

Read these sentences

	✓
Can you come to the beach with me?	
She had some sticky sweets in her bag.	
I can catch the train down to Redcar.	
They were happy to play in the team.	
I know the way to fix this problem.	
I wish that he could come to see me.	
Some days the pain gets me down.	
Do you know the way to the main street?	

TP Level 2.3 ☐

Progress check feedback

The Turning Pages Reading Levels show your Learner what they have achieved.

Congratulate them and explain what each level means.

Ask your Learner if there any sounds or words that they would like to go over again. Make a note of them below.

Go over them before moving on.

Your Learner has achieved the skills to read the light blue Turning Pages reading books, coded Level 2.3.

Tip:

Notes:

Congratulations!

You can read more vowel sounds and Sight Words as well as two-syllable words. You can now read more sentences.

You are now reading at **TP Level 2.3.**

Next we are going to look at:

- More vowel sounds
- More Sight Words
- Word endings

Listen and point

Learners are introduced to the **long ō** sound

1. Tell your Learner that the next long vowel sound they will learn about is **long ō**.
- Point to the two-letter combinations that make **long ō** on the Learner page: ***oa***, ***ow*** and say the sound.
- Explain that they are spelt differently but they both make the same **long ō** sound.
- Read the two lists of words emphasising the **long ō** sound.

2. Now go through the **oa** list with your Learner.
- Point to each word as you read it and ask your Learner to repeat the word.

3. Go through the same list at random. Say the words and ask your Learner to point to the correct word in each case.

4. Repeat these tasks with the **ow** list, gr**ow**.
- Point out that the **long ō** sound on the end of a word is often represented by ***ow*** and hardly ever by *oa* as in coc*oa*.

5. Read the other ways to represent the **long ō** shown at the bottom of the page. Explain that these will be covered later in the programme.

Tip: Always pronounce letters that make a long vowel sound as one sound, such as **long ō** in sl**ow**, b**oa**t.

Notes:

Listen and point

Find the words with the **long o** sound

The letters in bold say **long o**

oa	**ow**
b**oa**t	gr**ow**
fl**oa**t	fl**ow**
l**oa**n	sn**ow**
g**oa**t	bl**ow**
c**oa**t	sh**ow**
m**oa**n	cr**ow**
thr**oa**t	sl**ow**

Long o can also be spelt as: n**o**t**e**, s**ew**, t**oe**, th**ough**, n**o**

Listen

Learners listen and identify words with the **long ō** and **short o** sounds

Words to read

1. coat
2. top
3. soap
4. got
5. grow
6. float
7. slow
8. lock
9. oak
10. low

Tip: You may need to repeat the words more than once.

This task is not about spelling. Do the writing for your Learner.

1. Tell your Learner to listen to one word at a time and decide whether they can hear the **long ō** sound as in **blow** or **moan** or the **short o** sound as in **top**.

2. Say the word **coat** and sound it out: *c*-***oa***-*t*. Show how this has been recorded on the Learner page.

- Do the same with the word **top**: *t-o-p*. Show how this has been recorded.

3. Read the next word: **soap**. Sound out the word: *s*-***oa***-*p*. Say the word again. Ask your Learner:

- Which sound can you hear in the middle of the word s**oa**p? Is it **long ō** or **short o**?
- Ask your Learner to tick the correct column to show this.
- Write the word for your Learner in the left-hand column.
- Ask your Learner to read the word.

4. Do the same with all the other words.

Notes:

Listen

Listen for the **long o** and **short o** sounds

		Long **o**	Short **o**
		oa/ow	**o**
1.	c**oa**t	✓	
2.	top		✓
3.			
4.			
5.			
6.			
7.			
8.			
9.			
10.			

Listen and point

Learners listen and find the words with the **long ō** and the **short o** sounds.

Words to read

grow	pot
float	blow
chop	road
soak	lock
dot	glow
low	load

Tip: You may need to repeat the words more than once.

1. Tell your Learner that they will need to use their sounding out skills to find the word on the Learner page that matches what they hear.

2. Read the first word: **grow**. Sound it out *g*-*r*-***ow***. Say it again as a whole word. Ask your Learner:
   - What is the first sound you can hear? ***g***
   - What is the next sound you can hear? ***r***
   - What is the last sound you can hear? ***ow***

3. Ask your Learner to say the word again blending the sounds: **grow**.
   - Tell them to find the word **grow** in the grid and tick it.

4. Repeat this process with all the other words.

5. Ask your Learner to look at the words in the grid and to circle all the **long ō** sounds.

Notes:

Listen and point

Find the words with the **long o** and **short o** sounds

gr**ow**	l**oa**d	dot	gl**ow**
r**oa**d	chop	l**ow**	s**oa**k
bl**ow**	lock	fl**oa**t	pot

Read and check

Learners practise reading words with the **long ō** and the **short o** sounds

1. Ask your Learner to read each word in the grid on the Learner page.
   - Tell them to tick all the words they get right. Leave the others blank.

2. When your Learner has finished, go over any words that have not been ticked.
   - Read each of these words and sound them out.
   - Ask your Learner to read them again and to tick the ones they get right.

3. Make a note of any words that are still a problem in the Notes box.
   - Go over these words again once or twice.
   - If any words remain a problem, or take two or three tries to get right, add them to the blank column on page 81.

Tip: Point out that the **long *ō*** sound, spelt **ow** mostly comes at the end of words. We will look at the ***ow*** sound in words like h**ow** later on.

Notes:

Read and check

Check that you can read these words with **long o** and **short o** sounds

ow	✓
l**ow**	
sl**ow**	
bl**ow**	
thr**ow**	
m**ow**	
gl**ow**	
elb**ow**	
r**ow**	
sn**ow**	
sh**ow**	
st**ow**	
fl**ow**	

oa	✓
oat	
b**oa**t	
fl**oa**t	
s**oa**p	
oak	
m**oa**n	
thr**oa**t	
s**oa**k	
r**oa**d	
l**oa**d	
c**oa**t	
oath	

o	✓
pot	
plot	
stop	
lock	
chop	
notch	
mop	
rock	
block	
got	
cot	
dog	

Gap fill

Learners complete words that have a **long ō** sound: **ow, oa**

Words to read

ow	**oa**
slow	coat
throw	toast
flow	float
tow	coach
blow	roast
row	road
snow	soap
shown	moan
thrown	loaf

Tip: Cover up the grid not in use. This will help your Learner to focus on the task.

1. Ask your Learner to look at the grid on the left of the Learner page.
- Ask them to read the **long ō** sound in the heading: ***ow*** (as in sl***ow***).

2. Read the first word: **slow**. Sound it out: *s*-*l*-***ow***.
- Show your Learner how to complete the word using the letters given.
- Write in the letters and ask your Learner to read the whole word.

3. Take one word at a time in the **ow** list.
- Read it and sound it out.
- Ask your Learner to use the letters to complete the words in the grid. Encourage them to do the writing.
- You may need to repeat the words more than once.
- Use letter cards so that your Learner can move the letters around.

4. Complete the whole activity again with the words in the **oa** grid.

Notes:

Gap fill

Complete these words so that they make sense

ow	
s l	__ __ **ow**
th r	____ __ **ow**
f l	__ __ **ow**
t	__ **ow**
l b	__ __ **ow**
r	__ **ow**
n s	__ __ **ow**
n sh	____ **ow** __
r n th	____ __ **ow** __

oa	
t c	__ **oa** __
s t t	__ **oa** __ __
l t f	__ __ **oa** __
ch c	__ **oa** ____
s t r	__ **oa** __ __
d r	__ **oa** __
s p	__ **oa** __
n m	__ **oa** __
f l	__ **oa** __

Read and check

Learners practise reading words with the **long ō** sound: **ow, oa**

1. Ask your Learner to read each word in the grid.
- Tell them to tick all the words they get right. Leave the others blank.

2. When your Learner has finished, go over any words that have not been ticked.
- Read each of these words and sound them out.
- Ask your Learner to read them again and tick the ones they get right.

3. Make a note of any words that are still a problem in the Notes box.
- Go over these words again once or twice.
- If any words remain a problem, or take two or three tries to get right, add them to the blank column on page 85.

Tip: To help your Learner focus, cover up the column in the grid that your Learner is not reading.

Notes:

Read and check

Check that you can read these words with the **long o** sound: **ow, oa**

ow	✓
tow	
low	
blow	
slow	
grow	
flow	
stow	
show	
mow	
glow	
snow	
window	
sow	
elbow	

oa	✓
boat	
toast	
oats	
roast	
float	
bloat	
coast	
loaf	
groan	
road	
throat	
load	
soap	
coat	

Words from page 77	✓

Gap fill

Learners read sentences and fill in the missing words

1. Explain to your Learner they will read some sentences that have some words missing. They will choose the right words to complete the sentence.
   - Tell them that they may need to read each sentence more than once to get the meaning.

2. Read out Sentence 1 on the Learner page with the gaps and the words written in brackets:
   The wind may _______ the _______ on to the rocks. (**boats**, **blow**).
   - Show how to complete the sentence by trying each word from the brackets.
   - Write the correct words in the spaces.
   - Read the sentence again to help your Learner make sense of it:
     The wind may blow the boats on to the rocks.

3. Support your Learner to do the same with the other sentences. Read it with them if needed.
   - Each time ask your Learner to try both words to see which one makes sense.
   - Encourage your Learner to do the writing if they feel confident.

Tip: An ESOL Learner may need support to understand the meaning of each sentence. Read the sentences aloud and explain the meaning.

Notes:

Gap fill

Complete these sentences so that they make sense

1.	The wind may __________ the __________ on to the rocks.	b**oa**ts, bl**ow**
2.	J**oa**n __________ if she has to __________ the grass.	m**ow**, m**oa**ns
3.	The __________ tree fell on the __________ with a crash.	**oa**k, r**oa**d
4.	Which way is it to the __________ __________?	r**oa**d, c**oa**st
5.	The best pet at the __________ was Tom's __________.	sh**ow**, g**oa**t
6.	Sam could see a big __________ in its nest from his __________.	wind**ow**, cr**ow**
7.	The truck is __________ with such a big __________.	sl**ow**, l**oa**d
8.	I will put my thick __________ on to go out in this __________.	sn**ow**, c**oa**t

Read and check

Learners practise reading words with the **long ō** sound: **ow, oa**

1. Ask your Learner to read each word in the grid.
- Tell them to tick all the words they get right. Leave the others blank.

2. When your Learner has finished, go over any words that have not been ticked.
- Read each of these words and sound them out.
- Ask your Learner to read them again and tick the ones they get right.

3. Make a note of any words that are still a problem in the Notes box.
- Go over these words again once or twice.
- If any words remain a problem, or take two or three tries to get right, add them to the Parking page (page 111).

Tip:

Notes:

Read and check

Check that you can read these words with the **long o** sound: **ow, oa**

	✓
flow	
window	
boat	
roast	
crow	
blow	
stoat	
sow	
road	
moan	
show	
boast	
mow	
throat	

	✓
row	
float	
oath	
glow	
elbow	
oak	
soak	
toast	
grow	
roast	
tow	
coast	
snow	
blow	

Words from page 81	✓

Text and check

Learners read sentences that include words with the **long ō** sound: **ow, oa**

1. Point out that names start with a capital letter such as **B**en, **J**im, **J**oan, **S**am.

2. Ask your Learner to read the sentences and tick all the ones they get right.

3. Go over any sentences that have not been ticked.
   - Underline any errors in each sentence.
   - Read them to your Learner.
   - Support your Learner with two-syllable words if they need it. Use a finger to reveal the word bit by bit. Draw in the syllable break with a slash: **win/dows**.
   - Ask your Learner to read the sentences again and tick the ones they get right.

4. Make a note of any words that are a problem in the Notes box. Go over these words again once or twice.

5. If any words remain a problem, or take two or three tries to get right, add them to the Parking page (page 111).

Tip: Ask some questions about the sentences to check understanding such as: What did the crows eat? How long did Ben have a bad throat?

Notes:

Text and check

Read some sentences that have words with the **long o** sound: **ow, oa**

	✓
I will m**oa**n if this sn**ow** stops the train.	
I know that Ben's thr**oa**t has been bad for six days.	
The cr**ow**s fed on the seeds that Jim had s**ow**n.	
Come and help me r**ow** this b**oa**t to the beach.	
The wind bl**ow**s so fast off this bit of the c**oa**st.	
I can see a gl**ow** from some of the wind**ow**s.	
Sam hit his elb**ow** as he got his c**oa**t off the peg.	
A gr**oa**n went up as the sh**ow** had to stop.	
J**oa**n could not sit down on the l**ow** bench.	

Spot the word

Learners look for the Sight Words: **where**, **when**, **who**, **give**, **your**

This task relies on whole word recognition.

1. Read the words **where**, **when**, **who**, **give**, **your** on the Learner page.
   - Point out the words that begin with **wh**. They have different sounds at the beginning:
     - Where and when are pronounced with a ***w***.
     - Who is pronounced with ***h***.

2. Ask your Learner to read the words.
   - You may need to read them to your Learner more than once.

3. Show your Learner how to search the small boxes for the word **where**.
   - Tick the word every time you find it (there are 3). Write the number on the notepad.

4. Ask your Learner to search the small boxes for the word **when**.
   - Tick the word every time they find it (there are 3). Write the number on the notepad.

5. Do the same for the words: **who** (2), **give** (3), **your** (3).

Tip:

Notes:

Spot the word

Find these everyday Sight Words

where	when	who	give	your

give who when

your your

where when

when

who

your give

where where

give

where ____________

when ____________

who ____________

give ____________

your ____________

Read and check

Learners practise reading Sight Words

1. Remind your Learner that the Sight Words in the grid need to be remembered as whole words not sounded out.

2. Ask your Learner to read each word in the grid.
   - Tell them to tick all the words they get right and leave the others blank.

3. When your Learner has finished, go over any words that have not been ticked:
   - Read them to your Learner (do not sound them out).
   - Ask your Learner to read them again and tick the ones they get right.

4. If any words remain a problem, or take two or three tries to get right, write them in the Notes box and do 'Look and Say, Copy and Say' (as you do on the Parking page) until your Learner is confident.

Tip: The words **where** and **were** are similar-looking words. Point this out to your Learner.

Notes:

Read and check

Check that you can read these Sight Words

	✓
where	
when	
who	
give	
your	
come	
some	
where	
down	
when	
were	
give	
know	

	✓
who	
know	
your	
when	
come	
where	
down	
who	
some	
give	
were	
your	
were	

Text and check

Learners read sentences with Sight Words: **where**, **when**, **who**, **give**, **your**

1. Ask your Learner to read the Sight Words: **where**, **when**, **who**, **give**, **your**.
- Practise the words with your Learner if you need to.

2. Ask your Learner to read the sentences in the grid.
- Tick all the ones they get right and leave the others blank.

3. Go over any sentences that have not been ticked.
- Underline any errors in each sentence.
- Read them to your Learner.
- Ask your Learner to read the sentences again and tick the ones they get right.

4. Make a note of any words that are a problem in the Notes box. Go over these words again once or twice.

5. If any words remain a problem, or take two or three tries to get right, add them to the Parking page (page 111).

Tip: Ask some questions about the sentences to check understanding, such as: What went down? What will happen when you finish?

Notes:

Text and check

Read some sentences with Sight Words

where   when   who   give   your

	✓
Where have you been?	
Did you see who ran away?	
I will give you some cash when you finish.	
Where will this road lead to?	
Can you give me your address?	
Who would you put in your dream team?	
Where are my coat and my bag?	
I was there when the ship went down.	
We will come down to your show next week.	
Who has upset you?	
When does the bus get to Gatwick?	

Gap fill

Learners add endings **ed**, **ing** to words

1. Explain to your Learner that **ed** or **ing** can be added to some words to change the meaning or the tense. (Tense tells you if something is going on now, went on in the past or will go on in the future.)

2. Read Example 1: **rest**, **rested**, **resting**. Point out the root word: **rest** and the endings: **ed**, **ing**.
   - Ask your Learner to repeat the words.

3. Read Example 2: **back**, **backed**, **backing**. Point out that the **ed** ending is often pronounced as a ***t*** or ***d*** sound. Ask your Learner to listen to the words again to hear the difference: **rested**, **backed**. Tell them to read the words.

4. Ask your Learner to complete the **ed** column first by reading the root word and adding the ending: **ed**.
   - Ask them to read the completed word aloud.
   - Decide together how the end should be pronounced: ***ed***, ***t***, or ***d***.

5. Now ask your Learner to complete the words with the ending: **ing** and to read each word aloud.

Tip: Encourage your Learner to listen and decide for themselves which end sound is most suitable. **backed** pronounced as **back-ed** sounds wrong. Try **back-t** or **back-d**. ESOL Learners may need to be told.

Notes:

Gap fill

Use the endings **ed** and **ing** to complete these words

Example 1: **rest** | **rest + ed = rested** | **rest + ing = resting**

Example 2: **back** | **back + ed = backed** | **back + ing = backing**

Root word	+ ed	+ ing
fix	fix ____	fix _____
film	film ____	film _____
kick	kick ____	kick _____
land	land ____	land _____
help	help ____	help _____
risk	risk ____	risk _____
end	end ____	end _____
box	box ____	box _____

Listen and point

Learners listen for the **ed** ending

1. Read out the words across the top row of the grid on the Learner page.
   - Explain that although the ending **ed** is the same, the end sound is different: ***ed***, ***t*** or ***d***.
   - Ask your Learner to read the three words: **mended**, **mashed** and **rubbed**.

2. Read the other words in the grid at random and ask your Learner to point to the correct word in each case and repeat the word.

3. Reverse the process by pointing to random words and asking your Learner to read each one.
   - Encourage them to try out different ways to pronounce the ending before deciding which is correct.

4. Point out to your Learner that in some words the letter is doubled when adding these endings: sho**pp**ed, sla**mm**ed, sni**ff**ed. Remind your Learner that double letters make the same sound as a single letter.

Tip:

Notes:

Listen and point

Listen to words with the **ed** ending

mended	mashed	rubbed
trusted	sacked	begged
needed	sniffed	trained
toasted	tipped	played
handed	shopped	tanned
tested	matched	slammed

Read and check

Learners practise reading words with the **ed** ending

1. Ask your Learner to read each word in the grid on the Learner page.
- Tell them to tick all the words they get right. Leave the others blank.

2. When your Learner has finished, go over any words that have not been ticked.
- Read each of these words and sound them out.
- Ask your Learner to read them again and tick the words they get right.

3. Make a note of any words that are still a problem in the Notes box.
- Go over these words again once or twice.
- If any words remain a problem, or take two or three tries to get right, add them to the blank column on page 103.

Tip:

Notes:

Read and check

Check that you can read these words with the **ed** ending

	✓
kick**ed**	
pack**ed**	
rest**ed**	
train**ed**	
cash**ed**	
risk**ed**	
rust**ed**	
robb**ed**	
wish**ed**	
film**ed**	
roast**ed**	
kiss**ed**	

	✓
shopp**ed**	
rubb**ed**	
test**ed**	
play**ed**	
sack**ed**	
match**ed**	
lock**ed**	
need**ed**	
itch**ed**	
miss**ed**	
list**ed**	
stay**ed**	

Listen and point

Learners listen and identify words with the ending: **ing**

1. Read out the first word in the grid: **lifting**.
   - Ask your Learner to read the word.

2. Read the other words in the grid at random and ask your Learner to point to the correct word in each case and repeat the word.

3. Reverse the process by pointing to random words and asking your Learner to read each one.

4. Point out to your Learner that in some words the letter is doubled when adding these endings: sho**pp**ing, sla**mm**ing, sni**ff**ing. Remind your Learner that double letters make the same sound as a single letter.

Tip: There are rules about doubling letters when adding endings that apply to Learners when they are learning to spell but this is not important when reading.

Notes:

Listen and point

Listen to words with the ending: **ing**

lifting	mashing	rubbing
trusting	sacking	begging
needing	sniffing	training
toasting	tipping	playing
handing	shopping	tanning
testing	matching	slamming

Read and check

Learners practise reading words with the endings: **ed** and **ing**

1. Ask your Learner to read each word in the grid on the Learner page.
- Tell them to tick all the words they get right. Leave the others blank.

2. When your Learner has finished, go over any words that have not been ticked:
- Read each of these words and sound them out.
- Ask your Learner to read them again and tick the words they get right.

3. Make a note of any words that are still a problem in the Notes box.
- Go over these words again once or twice.
- If any words remain a problem, or take two or three tries to get right, add them to the blank column on page 107.

Tip:

Notes:

Read and check

Check that you can read these words with the endings **ed** and **ing**

	✓
kicked	
missed	
resting	
trained	
crashing	
seeming	
rusted	
robbed	
wishing	
filmed	
toasted	
kissing	

	✓
shopping	
played	
snowed	
playing	
sacked	
catching	
locking	
needed	
cleaning	
mashed	
listed	
stayed	

Words from page 99	✓

Gap fill

Learners read sentences and fill in the missing words

Your Learner may need to read each sentence more than once to get the meaning.

1. Explain to your Learner that they will read some sentences with one word missing from each sentence. They will choose the right word to complete the sentence.

2. Read out Sentence 1 with the gap and the words written in brackets:
He _______ the drums with a rock band. (**played**, **playing**).

- Show how to complete the sentence by trying each word from the brackets and deciding which one makes sense: **He played the drums with a rock band.**
- Write the correct word in the space.
- Read the sentence again to help your Learner make sense of it.

3. Support your Learner to do the same with the other sentences. Read it with them if needed.

- Each time ask your Learner to try both words to see which one makes sense.

Tip: An ESOL Learner may need support to understand the meaning of each sentence and to choose the correct word.

Notes:

Gap fill

Complete these sentences so that they make sense

1.	He ____________ the drums with a rock band.	played, playing
2.	It has been ____________ on the hills.	snowed, snowing
3.	The van ____________ into a tree.	crashed, crashing
4.	I went on a ____________ trip with my mum.	shopped, shopping
5.	She is ____________ on the bed.	rested, resting
6.	I am ____________ for the train to Bristol.	waited, waiting
7.	Sally ____________ that she would be rich.	dreamed, dreaming
8.	Perry ____________ his flight to Japan.	missed, missing

Read and check

Learners practise reading words with **ed** and **ing** endings

1. Ask your Learner to read each word in the grid on the Learner page.
- Tell them to tick all the words they get right. Leave the others blank.

2. When your Learner has finished, go over any words that have not been ticked.
- Read each of these words and sound them out.
- Ask your Learner to read them again and tick the words they get right.

3. Make a note of any words that are still a problem in the Notes box.
- Go over these words again once or twice.
- If any words remain a problem, or take two or three tries to get right, add them to the Parking page (page 111).

Tip:

Notes:

Read and check

Check that you can read these words with the endings **ed** and **ing**

	✓
lifting	
landing	
crashed	
trusted	
cleaning	
needed	
waiting	
mashing	
sacked	
snowing	
wished	
sniffing	

	✓
seemed	
rubbing	
shopping	
missed	
filmed	
testing	
tinned	
played	
topped	
raining	
tripped	
aiming	

Words from page 103	✓

Text and check

Learners read sentences that have words with the **ed** and **ing** endings

1. Ask your Learner to read the sentences in the grid.
   - Tick all the ones they get right and leave the others blank.

2. Go over any sentences that have not been ticked.
   - Underline any errors in each sentence.
   - Read them to your Learner and support them with words of more than one syllable if needed.
   - Read the word aloud as you tap the syllables out asking your Learner to tell you how many chunks (syllables) they hear you tap.
   - Ask them to draw in a slash for each syllable break, saying each chunk as they go along and then read the whole word again.
   - Ask your Learner to read the sentences again and tick the ones they get right.

3. Make a note of any words that are a problem in the Notes box. Go over these words again once or twice.

4. If any words remain a problem, or take two or three tries to get right, add them to the Parking page (page 111).

Tip: Ask some questions about the sentences to check understanding, such as: What did Len slip on? What did they film in my street?

Notes:

Read some sentences that have words ending with **ed** and **ing**

	✓
Len slipped on a wet patch and landed on his back.	
Wendy was waiting for the train to Ealing.	
I trusted her to finish the job.	
They filmed the TV show in my street.	
The fox was sniffing in the rubbish bin.	
I wished I had been trained for the job.	
He was running to catch the bus.	
He kissed her lips and wished her luck.	
The twins had matching hats.	

Parking page

Use the page opposite to note down any sounds or words you have come across in the manual that your Learner needs to practise again. Do this activity when you have completed all the other activities.

1. Write the words in the first (Park) column as you come across them in the manual.

2. When you and your Learner get to this page:
- Take **one** word at a time.
- Read it to your Learner and sound it out (Note: Sight Words are **not** sounded out.)
- Ask your Learner to read the whole word.
- Ask your Learner to copy the word and say it.
- Tick it if they get it right.
- Repeat the whole process with the same word. Copy and Say, Copy and Say until they are confident with it. Repeat on a new row if you need to.

3. Repeat the 'Look and Say, Copy and Say' process with all the other words in the Park column.

4. If your Learner continues to struggle with a word, make sure they know what the word means and try putting it into sentences for them.

Tip:

Notes:

Park. Look and Say	✓

Copy and Say	✓

Copy and Say	✓

Copy and Say	✓

Parking page

Use the page opposite to note down any words your Learner needs to practise again. Treat in the same way as outlined on the previous Parking page.

Tip:

Notes:

Parking page

Park. Look and Say	✓

Copy and Say	✓

Copy and Say	✓

Copy and Say	✓

Progress check

Explain to your Learner that this is a good point in the programme to see how things are going.

Ask your Learner to read each word in the Progress check.

- Tick everything they get right and leave the others blank.
- Use the Turning Pages Reading Levels to show your Learner how much they have achieved.
- Keep a note of any words or letter sounds they are not confident with. Your Learner can practise them at the beginning of the next session.

Turning Pages Reading Levels

All or most of the words with **long ō** read correctly. (No more than 5 errors.)	**TP Level 2.4**
All or most of the words with **ed** and **ing** endings read correctly. (No more than 5 errors.)	**TP Level 2.5**

Tip:

Notes:

Progress check

Read and tick all the words you know

Long o	✓
show	
coast	
road	
elbow	
oats	
low	
flow	
soap	
throat	
mow	

Long o	✓
snow	
loaf	
roast	
grow	
boat	
slow	
pillow	
load	
window	
oath	

TP Level 2.4 ☐

ed	✓
locked	
needed	
kicked	
wished	
shopped	
handed	
played	
roasted	
cashed	
rowed	

ing	✓
toasting	
testing	
lifting	
begging	
matching	
rubbing	
seeing	
sacking	
reaching	
showing	

TP Level 2.5 ☐

Progress check

Ask your Learner to read each sentence in the Progress check.

- Tick everything they get right and leave the others blank.
- Underline any errors in the sentences.
- Use the Turning Pages Reading Levels to show your Learner how much they have achieved.
- Keep a note of any words or letter sounds they are not confident with. Your Learner can practise them at the beginning of the next session.

Turning Pages Reading Levels

All or most of the words in the sentences read correctly. (No more than 5 errors.)	**TP Level 2.6**

If your Learner makes more than 15 errors overall (in both words and sentences) **you will need to go over the relevant activities again and spend some more time practising with the Turning Pages reading books. When you have done this, try the Progress check again.**

Tip:

Notes:

Progress check

Read these sentences

	✓
Who could eat some toast for tea?	
Can you give me a reading lesson?	
Tell me when the windows need cleaning next week.	
Come and sit down in my boat that is on the jetty.	
They know it will snow at the weekend.	
We were all crammed on the train to Kings Cross.	
Where can we put the wet coats?	
She trusted him to do the best job.	
He did my shopping and packed it away for me.	
He wished he was playing in the team.	
Your dog has been trained very well.	

TP Level 2.6 ☐

Progress check feedback

The Turning Pages Reading Levels show your Learner what they have achieved.

Congratulate them and explain what each level means.

Ask your Learner if there any sounds or words that they would like to go over again. Make a note of them below.

Go over them before moving on.

Your Learner has achieved the skills to read the light blue Turning Pages reading books, coded Level 2.6.

Tip:

Notes:

Congratulations!

You can read more vowel sounds and Sight Words as well as some word endings. You can now read longer sentences and Turning Pages reading books.

You are now reading at **TP Level 2.6.**

Next we are going to look at:

- More vowel sounds
- More Sight Words

Listen and point

Learners are introduced to the **long ī** sound

1. Tell your Learner that the next sound they will learn about is **long *ī***.
   - Tell them that this sound can also be represented by different letter combinations.
   - Point to the letter combinations that make **long *ī*: *igh*, *y*** and say the sound.
   - Explain that they are spelt differently but they both make the same **long *ī*** sound.
   - Read the two lists of words emphasising the **long *ī*** sound.
2. Now go through the **igh** list with your Learner.
   - Point to each word as you read it and ask your Learner to repeat the word.
3. Go through the same list at random, saying the words. Ask your Learner to point to the correct word in each case.
4. Repeat these activities with the other list: **y**
5. Read the other ways to represent the **long *ī*** shown at the bottom of the page. Explain that these will be covered later in the programme.

Tip: Point out to your Learner that the letter **y** can represent different sounds: **long *ī*** and **long ē.** Encourage them to try both sounds if they are not sure.

Notes:

Listen and point

Find the words with the **long i** sound

The letters in bold say **long i**

igh	y
h**igh**	tr**y**
s**igh**	fl**y**
l**igh**t	rel**y**
f**igh**t	suppl**y**
br**igh**t	m**y**
n**igh**t	sk**y**
r**igh**t	sl**y**

Long i can also be spelt as: l**i**k**e**, t**ie**, v**i**rus, h**eigh**t,

Listen

Learners listen and identify words with the **long ī** and **short i** sounds

Words to read

1. light
2. did
3. fright
4. try
5. bin
6. fly
7. sky
8. high
9. chip
10. night

Tip: You may need to repeat the words more than once.

This task is not about spelling. Do the writing for your Learner.

1. Tell your Learner to listen to one word at a time and decide whether they can hear the **long *ī*** sound as in h**igh** and m**y** or the **short *i*** sound as in w**i**n.

2. Say the word **ligh**t and sound it out: *l*-***igh***-*t*.

- Show how this has been recorded on the Learner page.
- Do the same with the word **did**: *d-i-d* and show how it has been written.

3. Read the next word: **fright**. Sound out the word *f-r-**igh**-t*. Say the word again. Ask your Learner:

- Which sound can you hear in the middle of the word fr**igh**t? Is it **long ī** or **short *i***?
- Ask your Learner to tick the correct column to show this.
- Write the word for your Learner in the left-hand column.
- Ask your Learner to read the word.

4. Do the same with all the other words.

Notes:

Listen

Listen for the **long i** and **short i** sounds

		Long i	Short i
		igh/y	i
1.	l**igh**t	✓	
2.	did		✓
3.			
4.			
5.			
6.			
7.			
8.			
9.			
10.			

Listen and point

Learners listen and identify words with the **long ī** and **short i** sounds

Words to read

might	try
light	rich
fright	high
fly	hid
my	slid
cry	this

Tip:

1. Tell your Learner that they will need to use their sounding out skills to find the word that matches what they hear.

2. Read the first word: **might**. Sound it out *m-**igh**-t*. Say it again as a whole word.
   Ask your Learner:
   - What is the first sound you can hear? ***m***
   - What is the next sound you can hear? ***igh***
   - What is the last sound you can hear? ***t***

3. Ask your Learner to say the word again blending the sounds: **might**.
   - Tell them to find the word **might** in the grid and tick it.

4. Repeat the process with all the other words.

5. Ask your Learner to look at the words and circle the **long *ī*** sounds: ***igh, y***

Notes:

Listen and point

Find the words with the **long i** and **short i** sounds

rich	m**igh**t	cr**y**	fr**igh**t
h**igh**	l**igh**t	m**y**	this
hid	tr**y**	slid	fl**y**

Read and check

Learners practise reading words with the **long ī** and **short i** sounds

1. Ask your Learner to read each word in the grid on the Learner page.
- Tell them to tick all the words they get right. Leave the others blank.

2. When your Learner has finished, go over any words that have not been ticked:
- Read each of these words and sound them out.
- Then ask your Learner to read it again and tick the ones they get right.

3. Make a note of any words that are still a problem in the Notes box.
- Go over these words again once or twice.
- If any words remain a problem, or take two or three tries to get right, add them to the blank column on page 131.

Tip: Point out that many of the words that use **igh** also have a **t** at the end such as **night**, **fright**. This can make it an easy pattern to spot in reading.

Notes:

Read and check

Check that you can read words with the **long i** and **short i** sounds

igh	✓
h**igh**	
s**igh**t	
r**igh**t	
s**igh**	
sl**igh**t	
n**igh**t	
l**igh**t	
fl**igh**t	
m**igh**t	
t**igh**t	
br**igh**t	
t**igh**t	

y	✓
tr**y**	
m**y**	
fl**y**	
sk**y**	
sp**y**	
appl**y**	
b**y**	
compl**y**	
rel**y**	
fr**y**	
sh**y**	
dr**y**	

i	✓
d**i**d	
r**i**ch	
p**i**n	
s**i**x	
b**i**g	
st**i**ck	
w**i**sh	
ch**i**n	
f**i**ll	
h**i**nt	
th**i**n	
th**i**s	

Gap fill

Learners complete words that have the **long ī** sound: **igh**, **y**

Words to read

igh	**y**
tight	try
flight	spy
high	cry
bright	dry
fright	my
might	shy
light	apply
sigh	sky

Tip: Cover up the grid not in use. This will help your Learner to focus on the task.

1. Ask your Learner to look at the grid on the left of the Learner page.

- Ask them to read the **long *ī*** sound in the heading: ***igh*** (as in h***igh***).

2. Read the first word: **tight**. Sound it out: *t*-***igh***-*t*.

- Show your Learner how to complete the word using the letters given.
- Write in the letters and ask your Learner to read the whole word.

3. Take one word at a time in the **igh** list.

- Read it and sound it out.
- Ask your Learner to use the letters to complete the words in the grid. Encourage them to do the writing.
- You may need to repeat the words more than once.
- Use letter cards so that your Learner can move the letters around.

4. Complete the whole activity again with the words in the **y** grid.

Notes:

Gap fill

Use the letters to complete words

igh	
t t	__ **igh** __
l f t	__ __ **igh** __
h	__ **igh**
r t b	__ __ **igh** __
r f t	__ __ **igh** __
t m	__ **igh** __
l t	__ **igh** __
s	__ **igh**

y	
r t	__ __ **y**
p s	__ __ **y**
c r	__ __ **y**
r d	__ __ **y**
m	__ **y**
sh	____ **y**
pp l a	__ ____ __ **y**
k s	__ __ **y**

Read and check

Learners practise reading words with the **long ī** sound: **igh**, **y**

1. Ask your Learner to read each word in the grid on the Learner page.
   - Tell them to tick all the words they get right. Leave the others blank.

2. When your Learner has finished, go over any words that have not been ticked.
   - Read each of these words and sound them out.
   - Ask your Learner to read them again and tick the ones they get right.

3. Make a note of any words that are still a problem in the Notes box.
   - Go over these words again once or twice.
   - If any words remain a problem, or take two or three tries to get right, add them to the blank column on page 135.

Tip:

Notes:

Read and check

Check that you can read words with the **long i** sound: **igh**, **y**

igh	✓
flight	
sigh	
night	
sight	
slight	
fight	
high	
plight	
right	
light	
fight	
might	
bright	
tight	

y	✓
my	
try	
why	
sty	
fly	
sky	
rely	
dry	
apply	
sly	
by	
fry	
cry	
shy	

Words from page 127	✓

Gap fill

Learners read sentences and fill in the missing words

Your Learner may need to read each sentence more than once to get the meaning.

1. Explain to your Learner they will read some sentences that have some words missing. They will choose the right words to complete the sentence.

2. Read out Sentence 1 with the gaps and the words written in brackets:
   I must _______ this lamp to see where I'm putting _______ feet. (l**igh**t, m**y**)
   - Show how to complete the sentence by trying each word from the brackets.
   - Write the correct words in the spaces.
   - Read the sentence again to help your Learner make sense of it:

   I must light this lamp to see where I'm putting my feet.

3. Support your Learner to do the same with the other sentences. Read it with them if needed.
   - Each time ask your Learner to try both words to see which one makes sense.

Tip: An ESOL Learner may need support to understand the meaning of each sentence. Read the sentence aloud and explain the meaning.

Notes:

Gap fill

Complete these sentences so that they make sense

1.	I must __________ this lamp to see where I'm putting __________ feet.	l**igh**t, m**y**
2.	We had such a __________ when the __________ began.	fr**igh**t, f**igh**t
3.	The __________ could be seen on the cliff top that __________.	l**igh**t, n**igh**t
4.	__________ as I __________ the cap would not come off.	m**igh**t, Tr**y**
5.	It was the __________ time for Jim to __________ for the job.	r**igh**t, appl**y**
6.	The __________ to Spain will __________ to set off at ten if the fog lifts.	fl**igh**t, tr**y**
7.	I don't think Liz will be __________ when she meets the __________ man.	r**igh**t, sh**y**
8.	I must be a __________ in this __________ outfit.	t**igh**t, s**igh**t

Read and check

Learners practise reading words with the **long ī** sound: **igh**, **y**

1. Ask your Learner to read each word in the grid on the Learner page.
- Tell them to tick all the words they get right. Leave the others blank.

2. When your Learner has finished, go over any words that have not been ticked:
- Read each of these words and sound them out.
- Ask your Learner to read them again and tick the words they get right.

3. Make a note of any words that are still a problem in the Notes box.
- Go over these words again once or twice.
- If any words remain a problem, or take two or three tries to get right, add them to the Parking page (page 161).

Tip:

Notes:

Read and check

Check that you can read these words with the **long i** sound: **igh, y**

	✓
right	
try	
sight	
sigh	
fry	
apply	
shy	
bright	
why	
shy	
blight	
plight	
cry	
high	

	✓
fight	
tight	
sly	
fright	
spy	
rely	
slight	
my	
by	
light	
dry	
flight	
sky	
shy	

Words from page 131	✓

Text and check

Learners read sentences that include words with the **long ī** sound: **igh**, **y**

1. Ask your Learner to read the sentences in the grid.
   - Tick all the ones they get right. Leave the others blank.

2. Go over any sentences that have not been ticked.
   - Underline any errors in each sentence.
   - Read them to your Learner.
   - Support your Learner with two-syllable words if they need it.
   - Point out that names start with a capital letter such as **S**pain.
   - Ask your Learner to read the sentences again and tick the ones they get right.

3. Make a note of any words that are a problem in the Notes box. Go over these words again once or twice.

4. If any words remain a problem, or take two or three tries to get right, add them to the Parking page (page 161).

Tip: Ask some questions about the sentences to check understanding, such as: What time is the flight to Spain? What colour is the coat being tried on?

Notes:

Text and check

Read some sentences that have words with the **long i** sound: **igh**, **y**

	✓
My fl**igh**t to Spain is at ten ton**igh**t.	
Sam had a fr**igh**t when the l**igh**ts went off.	
Liz went sh**y** and could not speak when the spotl**igh**t was on her.	
Can you tr**y** to dim that br**igh**t l**igh**t?	
May I tr**y** that cream coat on?	
The crow had to fl**y** h**igh** to reach its nest.	
I can see that it m**igh**t not be the r**igh**t time for you to be with us.	
I will have to reach up h**igh** to get that jug.	
I m**igh**t go on the coast road if it's all r**igh**t with you.	

Spot the word

Learners look for Sight Words: **call**, **want**, **here**, **after**, **before**

This task relies on whole word recognition.

1. Read **call**, **want**, **here**, **after**, **before** on the Learner page.
   - Ask your Learner to read the words.

2. Show your Learner how to search the small boxes for the word **call**.
   - Tick the word every time you find it (there are 4).
   - Write the number on the notepad.

3. Ask your Learner to search the small boxes for the word **want**.
   - Tick the word every time they find it (there are 3). Write the number on the notepad.

4. Do the same for the other words: **here** (3), **after** (2), **before** (3).

Tip: Point out **call** has the same spelling pattern as **all**. Your Learner can use this same spelling pattern to read the words: fall, tall, hall, small, wall and ball.

Notes:

Spot the word

Find these everyday Sight Words

call want here after before

want call before

here want

after call

call here

here after

before before

want call

call ____________

want ____________

here ____________

after ____________

before ____________

Read and check

Learners practise reading Sight Words

1. Remind your Learner that the Sight Words in the grid need to be remembered as whole words not sounded out.

2. Ask your Learner to read each word in the grid.
   - Tell them to tick all the words they get right. Leave the others blank.

3. When your Learner has finished, go over any words that have not been ticked:
   - Read them to your Learner (do not sound them out).
   - Ask your Learner to read them again and tick the ones they get right.

4. If any words remain a problem, or take two or three tries to get right, write them in the Notes box and do 'Look and Say, Copy and Say' (as you do on the Parking page) until your Learner is confident.

Tip:

Notes:

Read and check

Check that you can read these Sight Words

	✓
call	
want	
here	
after	
before	
know	
was	
who	
your	
where	
some	
before	
here	
after	

	✓
here	
before	
call	
give	
want	
come	
know	
saw	
want	
down	
she	
after	
call	
know	

Text and check

Learners read sentences with Sight Words

1. Ask your Learner to read the Sight Words: **call**, **want**, **here**, **after**, **before**.
   - Practise the words with your Learner if you need to.

2. Ask your Learner to read the sentences in the grid.
   - Tick all the ones they get right. Leave the others blank.

3. Go over any sentences that have not been ticked.
   - Underline any errors in each sentence.
   - Read them to your Learner.
   - Ask your Learner to read the sentences again and tick the ones they get right.

4. Make a note of any words that are a problem in the Notes box. Go over these words again once or twice.

5. If any words remain a problem, or take two or three tries to get right, add them to the Parking page (page 161).

Tip:

Notes:

Text and check

Read some sentences with Sight Words

call want here after before

	✓
I know what I want to do here.	
Clean up that mess before you go.	
You will get paid after you finish the job.	
We do not put meat in the curry here.	
I had to call him before the flight.	
Jan was in shock after the crash.	
I want you to call here on the way to the coast.	
Terry got out before the cash ran out.	
I want to get to know you.	
They want to own a flat here.	
Call them to the meeting after coffee.	

Listen and count

Learners count the number of sounds in words with the **ar** sound

Words to read

1.	part	p-ar-t	(3)
2.	sharp	sh-ar-p	(3)
3.	car	c-ar	(2)
4.	smart	s-m-ar-t	(4)
5.	star	s-t-ar	(3)
6.	arch	ar-ch	(2)
7.	arm	ar-m	(2)
8.	yard	y-ar-d	(3)
9.	party	p-ar-t-y	(4)

Tip: It may help to tap out the sounds: one tap for each sound. Encourage your Learner to do this. Make sure you sound out each sound in the word as shown in the word list. This will help your Learner to complete the gap fill.

This task is not about spelling. Do the writing for your Learner.

1. Ask your Learner to listen for the letter sounds.

- Read out the first word: **part**.
- Now sound out the word: *p*-***ar***-*t* (3 sounds).
- Point out the circle on the grid that shows the number of sounds in the word.
- Write the word and sound it out again pointing to the letters or letter combinations that make each sound.
- Point out the **ar** letter combination. Explain that these letters together represent ***ar***.

2. Read the next word to your Learner: **sharp** and then sound it out: *sh*-***ar***-*p*.

- Ask your Learner to circle the number of sounds they can hear in the word (3 sounds).
- Remind your Learner that ***sh*** also makes one sound.
- Write the word for your Learner, sound it out again and ask them to read the whole word by blending the sounds together.

3. Do the same with each of the other words.

Notes:

Listen and count

Count the number of sounds you can hear in each word

	The number of sounds				The whole word
1.	1	2	(3)	4	____________
2.	1	2	3	4	____________
3.	1	2	3	4	____________
4.	1	2	3	4	____________
5.	1	2	3	4	____________
6.	1	2	3	4	____________
7.	1	2	3	4	____________
8.	1	2	3	4	____________
9.	1	2	3	4	____________

Listen and point

Learners listen and find the words with the **ar** and **short a** sounds

Words to read

harm	army
far	had
chat	charm
scam	fact
scar	shark
hard	garlic
ham	shack
yard	harsh

Tip: Remember that some accents affect the way that these sounds are pronounced. This is fine as long as the short **a** and the **ar** sounds are clear.

1. Tell your Learner that they will need to use their sounding out skills to find the word that matches what they hear.

2. Read the first word: **harm**. Sound it out *h*-***ar***-*m*. Say it again as a whole word. Ask your Learner:

- What is the first sound you can hear? ***h***
- What is the next sound you can hear? ***ar***
- What is the last sound you can hear? ***m***

3. Ask your Learner to say the word again blending the sounds: **harm**.

- Tell them to find the word **harm** in the grid and tick it.

4. Repeat the process with all the other words.

5. Ask your Learner to look at the words in the grid and to circle all the ***ar*** sounds.

Notes:

Listen and point

Find the words with the **ar** and **short a** sounds

h**ar**m	chat	sc**ar**	sh**ar**k
had	g**ar**lic	ch**ar**m	h**ar**d
f**ar**	**ar**my	shack	y**ar**d
ham	scam	h**ar**sh	fact

Read and check

Learners practise reading words with the **ar** sound

1. Ask your Learner to read each word in the grid.
- Tell them to tick all the words they get right. Leave the others blank.

2. When your Learner has finished, go over any words that have not been ticked.
- Read each of these words and sound them out.
- Ask your Learner to read them again and tick the ones they get right.

3. Make a note of any words that are still a problem in the Notes box.
- Go over these words again once or twice.
- If any words remain a problem, or take two or three tries to get right, add them to the blank column on page 153.

Tip:

Notes:

Read and check

Check that you can read these words with the **ar** sound

	✓
c**ar**	
p**ar**k	
t**ar**	
m**ar**k	
st**ar**	
arch	
p**ar**ty	
st**ar**t	
y**ar**d	
sm**ar**t	
sh**ar**k	
arm	

	✓
h**ar**sh	
d**ar**k	
f**ar**m	
h**ar**d	
p**ar**t	
g**ar**lic	
sc**ar**	
c**ar**d	
sh**ar**p	
sc**ar**f	
h**ar**m	
g**ar**den	

Gap fill

Learners read sentences and fill in the missing words

1. Explain to your Learner they will read some sentences that have some words missing. They will choose the right words to complete the sentence.
   - Tell them that they may need to read each sentence more than once to get the meaning.

2. Read out Sentence 1 on the Learner page with the gaps and the words written in brackets:
   The _______ will not _______. (**start**, **car**).
   - Show how to complete the sentence by trying each word from the brackets.
   - Write the correct words in the spaces.
   - Read the sentence again to help your Learner make sense of it: **The car will not start.**

3. Support your Learner to do the same with the other sentences. Read it with them if needed.
   - Each time ask your Learner to try both words to see which one makes sense.

Tip: An ESOL Learner may need support to understand the meaning of each sentence. Read the sentences aloud and explain the meaning.

Notes:

Gap fill

Complete these sentences so that they make sense

1.	The ___________ will not ___________.	st**ar**t, c**ar**
2.	The ___________ left a ___________ on my leg.	sh**ar**k, sc**ar**
3.	It is ___________ to get into the ___________.	**ar**my, h**ar**d
4.	The pigs are kept in a ___________ at the ___________.	f**ar**m, b**ar**n
5.	You can ___________ your van in the ___________.	p**ar**k, y**ar**d
6.	I want to take ___________ in the ___________ match.	d**ar**ts, p**ar**t
7.	They had a ___________ in the ___________.	p**ar**k, p**ar**ty

Read and check

Learners read words with the **ar** sound

1. Ask your Learner to read each word in the grid.
- Tell them to tick all the words they get right. Leave the others blank.

2. When your Learner has finished, go over any words that have not been ticked.
- Read each of these words and sound them out.
- Ask your Learner to read them again and tick the ones they get right.

3. Make a note of any words that are still a problem in the Notes box.
- Go over these words again once or twice.
- If any words remain a problem, or take two or three tries to get right, add them to the blank column on page 157.

Tip:

Notes:

Read and check

Check that you can read these words with the **ar** sound

	✓
car	
dark	
part	
mark	
star	
hard	
party	
art	
harm	
smart	
bar	
start	

	✓
arm	
park	
farm	
harsh	
garden	
darts	
card	
march	
yard	
chart	
shark	
spark	

Words from page 149	✓

Word build

Learners make words with the **ar** sound

1. Ask your Learner to read the **sounds** of the letters at the top of the Learner page: ***c***, ***t***, ***d***, ***n***, ***p***, ***s***, ***ch***.
   - Explain to your Learner that they will use these letters with the ***ar*** sound to make words.

2. Show how to use the sounds to build the word **cart**, by sounding out the letters.
   - Sound out ***c-ar-t*** and write it down.

3. Work with your Learner to build other words that use the ***ar*** sound. The ***ar*** sound can be used at the beginning, the middle or the end of words.
   - Invite your Learner to write down the words or write the words for them.
   - Use letter cards so that your Learner can move the letters around. This hands-on approach helps learning.
   - Praise your Learner if they sound things out correctly even if they make non-words. Discuss these with your Learner.

4. If you are working with an ESOL Learner, you may need to tell them the words, and ask them to find the letters.

Tip: There are over 20 words that can be made using these letters with the sound ***ar***. Aim for at least 10. Your Learner can use the same letter twice in one word, such as **tart**.

Notes:

Word build

Make words using the letters and the **ar** sound

c t d n p s ch

_____ **ar** _____

_____ **ar** _____

_____ **ar** _____

_____ **ar** _____

_____ **ar** _____

_____ **ar** _____

_____ **ar** _____

_____ **ar** _____

_____ **ar** _____

_____ **ar** _____

_____ **ar** _____

_____ **ar** _____

_____ **ar** _____

_____ **ar** _____

_____ **ar** _____

_____ **ar** _____

Read and check

Learners read words with the **ar** sound

1. Ask your Learner to read each word in the grid.
- Tell them to tick all the words they get right. Leave the others blank.

2. When your Learner has finished, go over any words that have not been ticked.
- Read each of these words and sound them out.
- Ask your Learner to read them again and tick the ones they get right.

3. Make a note of any words that are still a problem in the Notes box.
- Go over these words again once or twice.
- If any words remain a problem, or take two or three tries to get right, add them to the Parking page (page 161).

Tip:

Notes:

Read and check

Check that you can read these words with the **ar** sound

	✓
arm	
card	
bar	
farm	
harsh	
mark	
far	
party	
army	
car	
chart	
yard	

	✓
part	
star	
harm	
harsh	
garden	
darts	
card	
march	
yard	
chart	
start	
spark	

Words from page 153	✓

Text and check

Learners read sentences using words with the **ar** sound

1. Ask your Learner to read the sentences in the grid.
   - Tick all the ones they get right. Leave the others blank.

2. Go over sentences that have not been ticked.
   - Underline any errors in each sentence.
   - Read them to your Learner.
   - Ask your Learner to read the sentence again and tick the ones they get right.

3. Make a note of any words that are a problem in the Notes box. Go over these words again once or twice.

4. If any words remain a problem, or take two or three tries to get right, add them to the Parking page (page 161).

Tip: Ask some questions about the sentences to check understanding such as: What did he get from his nan? What is their lucky charm?

Notes:

Text and check

Read some sentences using words with the **ar** sound

	✓
I had a hard time in the army.	
He went as far as he could by car.	
They play in the garden until it is dark.	
It was hard to part from Mark.	
He got a card and a Mars bar from his nan.	
You cannot park your car here.	
A spark set light to the hay in the barn.	
The star is my lucky charm.	
We had to march up and down the yard.	

Parking page

Use the page opposite to note down any sounds or words you have come across in the manual that your Learner needs to practise again. Do this activity when you have completed all the other activities.

1. Write the words in the first (Park) column as you come across them in the manual.

2. When you and your Learner get to this page:
- Take **one** word at a time.
- Read it to your Learner and sound it out (Note: Sight Words are **not** sounded out.)
- Ask your Learner to read the whole word.
- Ask your Learner to copy the word and say it.
- Tick it if they get it right.
- Repeat the whole process with the same word: Copy and Say, Copy and Say until they are confident with it. Repeat on a new row if you need to.

3. Repeat the 'Look and Say, Copy and Say' process with all the other words in the Park column.

4. If your Learner continues to struggle with a word, make sure they know what the word means and try putting it into sentences for them.

Tip:

Notes:

Parking page

Park. Look and Say	✓

Copy and Say	✓

Copy and Say	✓

Copy and Say	✓

Parking page

Use the page opposite to note down any words your Learner needs to practise again. Treat in the same way as outlined on the previous Parking page.

Tip:

Notes:

Park. Look and Say	✓

Copy and Say	✓

Copy and Say	✓

Copy and Say	✓

Progress check

Explain to your Learner that this is a good point in the programme to see how things are going.

Ask your Learner to read each word in the Progress check.

- Tick everything they get right.
- Leave blank any words that your Learner cannot read.
- Use the Turning Pages Reading Levels to show your Learner how much they have achieved.
- Keep a note of any words or letter sounds they are not confident with. Your Learner can practise them at the beginning of the next session.

Turning Pages Reading Levels

All or most of the words with **long *ī*** sound read correctly. (No more than 5 errors).	**TP Level 2.7**
All or most of the words with the ***ar*** sound read correctly. (No more than 3 errors).	**TP Level 2.8**

Tip:

Notes:

Progress check

Read and tick all the words you know

Long i	✓
light	
sky	
my	
high	
fright	
try	
shy	
right	
spy	
tight	

Long i	✓
dry	
by	
flight	
why	
fight	
cry	
sight	
bright	
fry	
sigh	

ar	✓
car	
hard	
army	
harsh	
chart	
card	
harm	
start	
mark	
yard	

TP Level 2.7 ☐

TP Level 2.8 ☐

Progress check

Ask your Learner to read all the words and sentences in the Progress check.

- Tick everything they get right.
- Underline any errors in the sentences.
- Use the Turning Pages Reading Levels to show your Learner how much they have achieved.
- Keep a note of any words or letter sounds they are not confident with. Your Learner can practise them at the beginning of the next session.

Turning Pages Reading Levels

All or most of the Sight Words read correctly. (No more than 4 errors.)	**TP Level 2.9**
All or most of the words in the sentences read correctly. (No more than 5 errors.)	**TP Level 3.0**

If your Learner makes more than 15 errors overall (in both words and sentences) **you will need to go over the relevant activities again and spend some more time practising with the Turning Pages reading books. When you have done this, try the Progress check again.**

Tip:

Notes:

Progress check

Read these Sight Words

	✓
come	
some	
down	
were	
know	

	✓
where	
when	
who	
give	
your	

	✓
call	
want	
here	
after	
before	

TP Level 2.9 ☐

Read these sentences

	✓
We have been down here before.	
He could not start his car that night.	
We were trying to get to your party after six.	
She helped me in hard times.	
Will you call to let us know when you can come?	
Who has got some sandbags to prop up the wall?	
Where can we give a helping hand?	
I have seen a green coat that I want for her wedding.	

TP Level 3.0 ☐

Progress check feedback

The Turning Pages Reading Levels show your Learner what they have achieved.

Congratulate them and explain what each level means.

Ask your Learner if there any sounds or words that they would like to go over again. Make a note of them below.

Go over them before moving on.

Your Learner has achieved the skills to read the light blue Turning Pages reading books, coded Level 3.0.

Tip:

Notes:

Congratulations!

You can now read more vowel sounds and Sight Words as well as two-syllable words and some word endings. You are now able to read more difficult Turning Pages reading books and sentences.

You are now reading at **TP Level 3.0.**

In the next (dark green) manual we are going to look at:

- More vowel sounds
- More Sight Words
- Some longer words
- Short forms of words